Founder's Pocket Guide: Startup Valuation

2nd Edition

1x1MEDIA

Simple, quick answers, all in one place.

By

Stephen R. Poland

1x1 Media
Asheville, North Carolina
United States

Care has been taken to verify the accuracy of information in this book. However, the authors and publisher cannot accept responsibility for consequences from application of the information in this book, and makes no warranty, expressed or implied, with respect to its content.

Trademarks: Some of the product names and company names included in this book have been used for identification purposes only and may be trademarks or registered trade names of their respective manufacturers and sellers. The author and publisher disclaim any affiliation, association, or connection with, or sponsorship or endorsement by, such owners.

ISBN 978-1-938162-04-6

© 2017 by 1x1 Media, LLC

email: info@1x1media.com

website : www.1x1media.com

Table of Contents

Founder's Pocket Guide: Startup Valuation

2nd Edition

"Embrace what you don't know, especially in the beginning, because what you don't know can become your greatest asset. It ensures that you will absolutely be doing things different from everybody else."

– Sara Blakely, SPANX founder

What the Founder's Pocket Guide Series Delivers

We developed the *Founder's Pocket Guide* series to provide quick answers to common questions encountered by entrepreneurs. Consider the following dilemmas:

> "I sort of know **what startup equity is**, but really don't understand the details, and I have an investor interested in my company. Where do I start?"

> "My co-founder said we need to **build a cap table to track our equity ownership**—how do we get started?"

> "My co-founders and I need to determine **how to divide the ownership** of our startup, but how can we be certain we get it right?"

> "I've heard that **convertible debt is a good funding structure for early-stage startups**. What is convertible debt and how do I approach potential investors with a funding pitch?"

The *Founder's Pocket Guide* series addresses each of the topics in a concise and easy to reference format.

Look for these current titles at www.1x1media.com:

- *Founder's Pocket Guide: Founder Equity Splits*

- *Founder's Pocket Guide: Cap Tables*

- *Founder's Pocket Guide: Convertible Debt*

- *Founder's Pocket Guide: Terms Sheets and Preferred Shares*

- *Founder's Pocket Guide: Friends & Family Funding*

Disclaimers

The content in this guide is not intended as legal, financial, or tax advice and cannot be relied upon for any purpose without the services of a qualified professional. With that disclaimer in mind, here's our position on how to best use the guidance provided in this work.

Great entrepreneurs use all the resources available to them, making the best decisions they can to mitigate risk and yet move ahead with the most important tasks in their roadmaps. This process includes consulting lawyers, CPAs, and other professionals with deep domain knowledge when necessary.

Great entrepreneurs also balance a strong do-it-yourself drive with the understanding that the whole team creates great innovations and succeeds in bringing great products to the world. Along those lines, here's a simple plan for the scrappy early-stage founder who can't afford to hire a startup lawyer or CPA to handle all of the tasks needed to close a funding deal or form the startup:

> **1. Educate yourself on what's needed.** Learn about startup equity structures and issues, legal agreements, financing structures, and other company formation best practices, and then;

> **2. Get your lawyer involved**. Once you thoroughly understand the moving parts and have completed some of the work to the best of your ability, pay your startup-experienced lawyer or other professional to advise you and finalize the legal contracts.

With this self-educating and money-saving sequence in mind, let's dig in to this *Founder's Pocket Guide*.

In This Pocket Guide

For many early-stage entrepreneurs assigning a pre-money valuation to your startup is one of the more daunting tasks encountered during the fundraising quest. This guide provides a quick reference to all of the key topics around early-stage startup valuation and provides step-by-step examples for several valuation methods.

The guidance and valuation methods detailed here are suited for early-stage, pre-revenue, or early-revenue ventures. Founders seeking information on later-stage company valuation methods should consult a CPA or other valuation specialists trained in quantitative valuation methods.

This *Founder's Pocket Guide* helps startup founders learn:

- **What a startup valuation is** and when you need to start worrying about it.

- **Key terms and definitions** associated with valuation, such as pre-money, post-money, and dilution.

- **How investors view the valuation task**, and what their expectations are for early-stage companies.

- **How the valuation fits with your target raise amount** and resulting founder equity ownership.

- How to do **the simple math for calculating valuation percentages.**

- How to **estimate your company valuation** using several accepted methods.

- What **accounting valuation methods** are and why they are **not well suited for early-stage startups.**

Founder Pro Tips

 To further help guide you through the ins and outs of early-stage startup valuations, you'll find useful tips throughout this guide that provide deeper insights, insider tips, and additional explanations.

Download the Startup Valuation Explorer File

Be sure to download our **Startup Valuation Explorer**™ file to follow along with key examples reviewed in this guide. With a live version of the Excel file you'll be able to test various valuation "what-if's" and document your work of determining a reasonable pre-money valuation for your startup.

Grab the free worksheet here:

<u>http://www.goo.gl/LZSVVV</u>

1

Valuation Fundamentals

In this section we'll review the fundamentals of early-stage startup valuations including terminology, basic valuation calculations, common valuation pitfalls, how to talk to investors about your company valuation estimates.

How to Think About Startup Valuation

To get started, let's review some of the basic ideas of early-stage startup valuation.

- At the very early stages of your startup the company has very little value.

- As you accomplish milestones in your startup (build product, get customers) the value of your company increases.

- If you are working to raise money from investors (equity funding), founders trade a portion of their ownership for cash investment.

- The investment amount raised from investors and the valuation of your company determines how much equity ownership you give up to the investors.

- There are no exact formulas for determining early-stage valuations.

- The valuation of your company is established by agreement between you and the investor.

- Investors want a low valuation (before they put their money in).

- Founders want a high valuation.

All of these factors point us to the first rule of early-stage startup valuation:

The First Rule of Startup Valuation

Your startup is worth whatever **you** and the **investor** **agree** it's worth.

Therefore, it is your job as the startup founder to develop a reasonable valuation range that investors will accept. With this key rule in mind let's continue to dig in.

Valuation Increases at Each Stage of Equity Funding

As your startup makes progress, launches its products, adds new customers, and streamlines supporting operations, it is reducing the risk associated with the startup surviving and ultimately succeeding. This risk reduction adds value to the startup and at each round of equity funding that value should be growing. Along the way, as outside investors buy into the startup, founders give up a portion of their equity to the investors.

The graphic below shows an example progression of declining founder ownership percentages and increasing valuation as the startup matures and raises more outside equity investment. While the founder ownership percentage is getting diluted at each funding event, the overall valuation of the startup is increasing; therefore the founder's portion of ownership is worth more

Valuation and Founder Equity

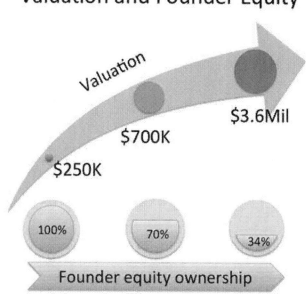

The following table shows an example progression of funding stages, investor types, and valuations of a typical startup. Early stages of the startup are funded the by the founder or friends and family, and the investments do not require a valuation to be established. Later stages require more funding from angels and venture capitalists, resulting in equity deals and the need to establish and grow the valuation of the startup.

Startup Stage	Investors	Investment Type	Investment Amount	Valuation
1. Idea Stage	Founders Round	Personal Funds	$50,000	Not needed
2. Product Developed	Friends & Family Round	Simple Loan	$30,000	Not needed
3. Early Customers	1st Angel Round	Convertible Note	$150,000	Not needed
4. Traction	2nd Angel Round	Equity	$250,000	$1,500,000
5. Scaling	VC Round 1 (Series A)	Equity	$1,500,000	$4,000,000
6. Rapid Growth	VC Round 2 (Series B)	Equity	$3,000,000	$9,500,000

A Good Sign

If you are discussing your startup's valuation with investors it means a lot of other things are right: large market size, great team, IP on track, milestones achieved, good exit potential, and so on.

Most investors need check marks in the yes column on these items before they consider letting go of cash.

If these things are not right, or at least repairable, then investing at even a low valuation does not make sense for the investor.

Valuation and Funding Terminology

Now that you understand the basics and why valuation is needed, let's review several additional key terms associated with startup funding and valuations:

- **Pre-money Valuation.** The value placed on a startup before an investment round. The pre-money valuation is a key point of negotiation between founders and equity investors.

- **Post-money Valuation.** The value of the startup after the investment round. The investment amount + the pre-money valuation = the post-money valuation.

- **Founder Dilution.** The amount of ownership given up by startup founders, expressed as a percentage— "the founders are willing to accept a 20% dilution in exchange for a $200,000 angel fund investment."

- **Investor Dilution.** Founders are not the only stakeholders that give up equity as new investors come into the funding picture. Existing investors can also be required to withstand a reduction in their ownership percentage in the startup. If the startup raises multiple rounds of equity investment, early investors will give up some ownership to new investors. Anti-dilution rights attached to preferred shares are one way investors attempt to limit their exposure to dilution.

- **Raise or Round (Investment Round).** The process and result of raising money for your startup is called a round or a raise. Whether you are at the beginning stages of the money raising process, or put investor money in the bank, each round is given a name or designation, such as Seed round or Series A round.

- **Priced Round.** Agreeing with investors on the valuation of the startup, and therefore the price per share of stock can be calculated. Also called pricing the company.

- **Down Round.** When founders accept an equity investment at a valuation lower than the previously established valuation. The company is worth less now than it was at the previous investment round. See the section "Understanding Down Rounds" later in this guide for more details.

- **Seed Round.** In common usage, a seed round can be any investment in a startup used to start the company and create its first products or services. Money coming from the founders themselves, friends and family, or other support associated with the entrepreneurs that are starting the company can all qualify as a seed round.

- **Series A, Series B, etc.** Series A is a term used to mean many things, but typically, a Series A is the first Venture Capital level investment round. Additional investments from institutional investors follow the same pattern, Series B, Series C, and so on. Also note that VCs are in the business of investing other institutions money, not personal money, as is the case from angels or friends and family investors.

- **Equity.** The ownership of the startup—who owns how much. In the most common sequence, the founders own 100% equity of the startup at formation, then give up chunks of ownership to outside investors in exchange for cash investments. Portions of equity are also given to key employees in the form of stock options as additional compensation for their contributions to the startup's efforts.

When to Worry About Valuation

So when do you need to establish a pre-money valuation of your company? To answer this question, let's take a look at a number of events or milestones signal the need to begin thinking about your startup's valuation:

Developing Your Funding Plan. What kind of startup are you building and when will you need outside investors? The nature of your startup determines how soon you will seek outside equity funding, and consequently, the need to establish valuations at each funding round. For example, high growth startups like biotech focused startups typically require several rounds of funding to bring their products to market, relying on angels and VCs to invest over several years. While it will likely change along the way, many founders create a funding roadmap by planning the major stages of the startup's growth and estimating how much money is needed at each funding round.

Starting Equity Investor Discussions. Scheduling investor meetings and making funding pitches drives the need to establish a pre-money valuation of your startup. While funding structures such as convertible debt can be used to delay the need to establish your valuation, most angel investors are likely to push you to give at least a ball park range for your startup's pre-money valuation.

Establishing a Stock Incentive Plan. Many startups set aside a pool of stock options to be used to reward early employees for taking on the risk of joining a startup, and to offset lower than market rates for salaries and other benefits. Stock option pools influence the overall ownership picture of the startup (tracked in a capitalization table) and should trigger valuation discussions among the founders. While

17

stock options do not directly influence the valuation of the startup, they are calculated into the number of fully diluted shares outstanding, and therefore affect ownership percentages of all shareholders.

Equity Split Discussions Among Co-Founders. One of the essential steps in startup formation is establishing the ownership split when the startup has multiple startup founders. Before entering discussions with outside investors like angels or VCs, founders should have a clear agreement on who owns how much of the new venture. Two questions need attention prior to taking on new investors: 1. What is the equity split between founders—50%/50%, 20%/20%/60%, and so on, and 2. What is the pre-money valuation of the company?

The Basic Valuation Equation

In this section we get into the basic math that links your valuation, funding raise amount, and the amount of equity investors get for their money.

Before outside investors enter the picture, founders own 100% of the equity in the startup. The investor will buy a part of that ownership via the invested cash. For example, if the investor agrees to invest $1,000,000 in the startup, how much ownership (equity) does that buy?

You can calculate the answer in a simple sequence:

1. *Assign a value to the startup before the investment dollars are injected.* This value is called the pre-money valuation of the startup.

2. *Add the investment amount to the pre-money valuation.* The result is called the post-money valuation.

3. *Divide the investment amount by the post-money valuation to give the equity percentage owned by the investors.* This percentage is also called the founder's dilution amount or percentage.

The following equation with example valuation and investment amounts shows how pre-money and post-money fit together.

PRE-MONEY VALUATION **$2** MILLION + INVESTMENT AMOUNT **$1** MILLION = POST-MONEY VALUATION **$3** MILLION

You will use this basic valuation equation over and over again to calculate the impact of investments in your company on ownership shares.

Investors are motivated to negotiate lower pre-money valuations that result in larger percentage ownership percentages. The larger percentage of equity the investor gets for his/her money, the greater return the investor will realize if the startup gets acquired for a large amount of money.

Calculating Investor Ownership Percentage (or Founder Dilution)

To better understand the connection between your pre-money valuation and the equity amount the investor gets for his money, consider the following example.

Your startup uses a few valuation methods (detailed later in this guide) and establishes a $1,250,000 pre-money valuation. During your fundraising efforts, you convince an angel group to invest $250,000 in your venture, but they negotiate the pre-money valuation down to an even $1,000,000. The valuation equation flows like this:

$$
\begin{array}{lr}
\text{Pre-Money Valuation} & \$\,1{,}000{,}000 \\
+\ \text{Raise Amount} & \underline{\$\quad 250{,}000} \\
\text{Post-Money Valuation} & \$\,1{,}250{,}000
\end{array}
$$

The percentage equity owned by investors after the funding round closes is expressed by this simple equation:

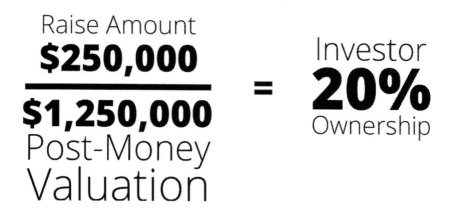

In our example the investors will own 20% of the startup after the group's investment.

The ownership percentage can be thought of as either giving the equity percentage to the investors, or taking it away (dilution) from the founders. Either way, the calculation is the same.

Expressing Your Valuation and Raise Amount to Investors

There are two approaches to use when talking to investors about your fundraising goals and the valuation of your startup. You can either express the amount of dilution you are willing to give up for the investment raise, or you can express your desired pre-money valuation and raise amount. The following sections illustrate the options.

Implied Valuation

Founders working to raise equity funding from investors are eventually confronted with two key investor questions:

1. How much of an investment does the business need in this round, and;

2. How much equity are you willing to give up for the investment?

The answer to these questions also answers a third key question on the investor's mind:

3. What is your valuation?

Let's walk through the calculations with the following example.

1. *Express your raise amount and equity expectation.* Talking about your raise amount and equity exchange is often expressed in the following manner:

We are raising **$150,000** for **15%** of the company.

This statement implies a **post-money** valuation of $1,000,000. Why?

Here you are stating your starting point for the pre-money valuation, $1.5 million, and saying you are willing to give up 15% for the $150,000 investment. With a little mental math, this statement **implies** the valuation you are placing on your startup. Step 2 shows the simple math.

2. *Calculate the Implied Post-Money Valuation.* Divide the raise amount by the equity ownership percentage (expressed as a decimal), resulting in the post-money valuation, or how much you are saying your company is worth after the investor injects cash into the venture.

Raise Amount

$$\frac{\$150,000}{.15} = $$ Post-Money Valuation $1,000,000

Equity Percentage

3. **Calculate the Pre-Money Valuation.** Subtract the raise amount from the post-money valuation giving the pre-money valuation, or how much you are saying your company is worth before the investor injects cash into the venture.

Post-Money Valuation	**$ 1,000,000**
− Raise Amount	**$ 150,000**
Pre-Money Valuation	**$ 850,000**

Implied Founder Dilution

In a similar fashion as the implied valuation discussion above, some founders prefer to talk to investors about their valuation in terms of their raise amount and their target pre-money valuation.

Let's look at an example of this approach.

1. **Express your raise amount and pre-money valuation.** Talking about your raise amount and valuation can be expressed in the following manner:

We are raising **$500,000** on a pre-money valuation of **$1,000,000**.

2. ***Calculate the post-money valuation.*** Simply add the raise amount to the stated pre-money valuation, resulting in the post-money valuation, or how much you are saying your company is worth after the investor puts cash into the venture.

Pre-Money Valuation **$ 1,000,000**
+ Raise Amount **$ 500,000**
Post-Money Valuation **$ 1,500,000**

3. ***Calculate the implied dilution percentage.*** Divide the raise amount by the post-money valuation, giving the founder dilution percentage, or how much equity founders are willing to give the investors in exchange for the cash injected into the startup venture.

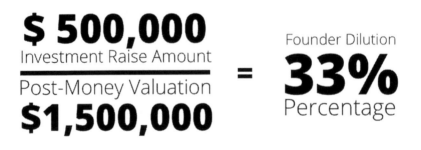

$ 500,000
Investment Raise Amount
—————————————
Post-Money Valuation
$1,500,000

=

Founder Dilution
33%
Percentage

Remember that the founder dilution percentage is also the amount of equity the new investors will be buying with their cash.

Valuation and Raise Amount Sanity Check

The amount of funding you seek from equity investors must also make sense in relationship to your pre-money valuation.

Consider the equation:

$$\frac{\text{Pre-Money Valuation}}{2} = \text{Maximum Raise}$$

Dividing your pre-money valuation by two gives you a good ballpark limit for how much you can raise in a particular funding round. The math works out so that the investor would own 33% of the equity after the investment. Note this is a simplified guideline. Option pools and other factors can change the ownership math.

Early-Stage Valuation Pitfalls

The following list summarizes several pitfalls to avoid when establishing the valuation of your startup.

Too Early. In this scenario, a founder may decide to enter into an equity deal very early in the life of the startup with a friends and family investor, such as a parent or wealthy uncle. For example, rich Uncle Larry offers to invest $20,000 for a 20% share of the company, and you and your co-founder are just fleshing out the startup idea. The 20% share in exchange for $20,000 implies a valuation of $100,000 (100% / 20% = 5, and 5 x $20,000 = $100,000). If the startup then requires additional funding rounds from experienced investors, it may be difficult for the founders to explain why Uncle Larry owns such a large percentage for only $20,000. Such early stage startups are better off raising capital in the form of friends and family loans, crowd funding like Kickstarter, or perhaps convertible debt.

Too High, Too Early. Founders occasionally encounter enthusiastic (inexperienced) investors willing to value the startup at high levels early in the startup's lifecycle. For example, establishing a $4,000,000 valuation for an idea-stage startup with no paying customers and an inexperienced founding team falls into the too high, too early category. If the startup requires additional investment rounds, the high early valuation increases the chances of a down-round valuation, or more likely, no funding at all from experienced investors.

Lack of Customer Validation. Many investors expect an early-stage startup to be engaged with potential customers, even if working versions of the product are still under development. Having actual customers validates that the product solves a significant problem and customers are willing to pay for it, which is the Holy Grail sought by investors (and founders alike.) Establishing a sizable valuation prior to building a customer track record is a mistake to be avoided at all costs.

Valuing the Idea or Market Potential. The startup team and the milestones achieved in a startup should be at the core of all valuations. Having experienced founders with prototypes developed, technology proven, paying customers, IP issued, skilled team recruited, and so on matters; these milestones add real value to a new venture. In contrast, ideas, business plans, and forecasted market sizes in themselves offer little value to investors. Think twice before assigning a valuation to an idea-stage venture and pitching to investors.

Raise Amount, Equity, and Valuation Disconnect. Consider a rookie mistake occasionally committed by first time entrepreneurs. A first timer might say something like, "We are seeking $250,000 for 5% of our company," not realizing that this request implies a valuation of $5,000,000. (There are twenty 5%'s in 100%, right. So if one 5% is worth $250,000, then 20 x $250,000 = $5,000,000). Be sure to do the math and connect your raise amount with your pre-money valuation.

Over Optimizing Your Valuation. Experienced startup founders learn to accept valuations that are "within range" of the value they are seeking. Spending too much time trying to negotiate the highest possible valuation with investors wastes time and can indicate an inexperienced founder. Higher valuations translate into less founder dilution, but many other factors have a bigger influence on the overall outcome of the startup, such as proving customers care about your products. Giving up a few additional percentage points of ownership to close an investment deal and get back to the business of the startup is usually the best move.

Fixating on Valuation Only. Founders often focus too much on negotiating a high pre-money valuation when raising money from angel investors. In reality, there are many additional deal points that influence how much control and potential exit proceeds founders will end up with in an investment deal. For example, preferred share rights like liquidation preferences, voting rights, and board of director seats are often more important to the founders than just a high valuation number. Check out the *Founder's Pocket Guide: Term Sheets and Preferred Shares* for complete details on how the numerous term sheet elements can influence your fundraising deal with angel investors.

 ### Delaying the Need to Establish a Valuation

Startup founders often benefit by delaying the need to place a value on their startup, and yet still need startup capital from outside investors. Without meaningful accomplishments achieved, pricing the startup often disadvantages founders. With few actual achievements, founders often feel pressured to accept a low valuation, resulting in heavy dilution early in the startup's life. If founders give up too much, too early, they might become unmotivated. Finding other ways to fund the startup, such as friends and family loans or crowd funding enables the founders to achieve notable milestones and delay setting the valuation of the company.

What is a Down Round?

When founders accept an equity investment at a valuation lower than the previously established valuation, a down round has occurred. In other words, the company is worth less now than it was at the previous investment round.

Most down rounds happen because the startup is running out of cash. In order to keep the startup alive, founders go back to the well and ask either existing investors or new investors to inject more cash into the business. In this situation, if the startup has not reached significant milestones that point to a higher valuation, investors can argue that the startup's valuation is either flat (the same as the previous round) or down (lower than the previous round.) To close the investment deal, founders will accept more dilution in exchange for more cash to keep the startup alive.

The motivations of investors in down round situations vary, but in most cases, the investors still see promise in the startup and are willing to risk additional cash to keep the startup alive.

The causes and effects of a down round include issues like these:

> **Raising Too Much, Too Early.** If founders raise a very large initial funding round (in the millions), it can be almost impossible to gain enough traction to justify a higher valuation the next time around. Valuation and raise amount are always coupled and founders should seek to balance to two by setting conservative goals for milestone achievement.

> **Burn Rate Too High.** A high monthly burn rate coupled to delayed milestone achievement results in entrepreneurs holding out their hands to investors to

ise additional funding. With leverage favoring the
investors, the investors can argue for a flat valuation
(ot higher or lower), and force founders to accept
more equity dilution of a down round.

Founder Motivation. Any time a startup takes on
new equity investors, existing shareholders get
diluted. Down rounds are no different—founders
are diluted when new cash is injected at a level or
reduced valuation. If founders face too much dilution,
they can lose motivation to follow through with
building the startup entirely. Unmotivated founders
are death to a startup.

Effects on Employees and Other Stakeholders.
Down rounds also affect the morale and motivation
of employees, especially option holders. Reducing
the valuation of the startup also reduces the value
(on paper anyway) of stock options. While the cash
injected from the down-round investment enables the
startup to live on, founders can find it challenging to
keep employees motivated.

Determining Early Stage Pre-money Valuations

So how do you determine what a reasonable pre-money
valuation is for your startup?

Numerous factors influence how investors view what a fair
pre-money valuation should be for your startup. Many of
these factors are used (and assigned value) in the valuation
methods detailed later in this guide.

Below is a list of several valuation factors floating around
the head of the typical investor. As you review the list, think
about your startup and take inventory of the factors that will

influence your pre-money valuation.

In the next section, "Early-stage Valuation Methods", you will see how all these factors come into play when estimating a pre-money valuation for your startup.

Company Factors

These valuation-influencing factors relate directly to the startup itself.

- **Founders and Team.** How experienced is the founding team? Have they worked on a startup before, or is this their first go?

- **Market Size.** How big is the market the startup is going after? Do large players already dominate the overall market or is it large enough to support many competitors?

- **Revenue Projections.** What are the revenue projections over the next three to five years? Is the amount of revenue reasonable in relationship to the market size estimates?

- **Technology or Market Solution.** Does the technology or product offer a significant advantage to customers/users, or is it merely a nice to have option?

- **Competition.** What is the competition like in the startup's business or market sector? Does your startup have a significant way to differentiate itself from the competition?

- **Intellectual Property (IP).** Does the startup have significant IP (patents, trade secrets, trademarks) or other strong competitive advantages?

- **Customer Traction.** Do you have paying customers or numerous users signing up? At what rate can you add new ones? How much does it cost you to acquire a new customer compared to the lifetime value of that customer?

- **Exit Potential.** Is it reasonable to believe that the startup can achieve enough success, attracting large acquisition partners, resulting in a large multiple buyout within five to seven years?

- **Board of Directors and Advisors.** Have the founders assembled an experienced advisory team that can help them enter their primary market segments? Does the formal board of directors augment the founding team, filling gaps and increasing the possibility of success?

Deal Factors

These factors relate to how investor views the financial and control attractiveness of the investment deal.

- **Pre-Money Valuation and Investment Amount.** Does the pre-money valuation and investment amount align with the investor's expectations for equity ownership? That is, will they own a large enough percentage of the startup to offset the risk they are taking with their cash investment?

- **Term Sheet Deal Points.** Will the investor get preferred share rights that make the investment deal less risky? Items include investor control rights like board of director seats, voting rights on key decisions, and so on.

- **Amount Already Invested.** How much money has already been invested in the startup, and how much time in terms of development, research, or innovation has been accumulated?

- **Stage of the Startup.** What stage of development is the startup at: idea/business plan, product developed and tested, or beyond?

- **Need for Additional Investment.** Does the startup need a significant amount of additional cash to reach its goals? How likely is it the startup can raise the additional funding needed in the future?

Macro Environment Factors

These factors shed light on how investors think about issues that are external and often uncontrollable by the startup.

- **Industry trends.** Is the industry and market of the startup growing, level, or shrinking? Are there industry trends (like automation or cloud-based services) that could either hurt or help the prospects for the startup's success?

- **Economy.** What is the current economy like? Is the country in a recession, or is the economy growing. Are there more attractive investment options for the investor's cash in the stock market?

- **Political.** Are there political changes that could influence the outcome of an investment deal? Changes in taxes credits and deductions have a heavy influence on how angel investors view startup investing.

- **Regulatory.** Are there federal, state, or local regulations that could affect the startup or it's market.

Local Environment Factors

Local environment factors are the "close to home" topics that can influence how investor views the valuation task.

- **Comps.** Short for "comparables", comps are the similar startups in your local or regional area. Have they been successful in raising startup funding? Does your startup have notable differences from these comps? See the section Market Comp valuation method for more details for how to size up your startup compared to similar startups in your space.

- **Recent exits.** Are there companies similar to yours that have recently been acquired? Investors often view a similar company exit as a huge validation. "If they can do it, maybe you can too." On the other hand, if the investors view your startup as very similar to yours, they might feel like the acquired startup won the race already.

- **Saturation.** How many high quality, investable, startups are there competing for the limited amount of investor dollars in your local area.

With all these factors considered, let's move on to the next section "Early Stage Valuation Methods" to incorporate these factors into building a valuation estimate for your startup.

2

Early Stage Valuation Methods

This section details several methods for estimating a pre-money valuation for your startup.

To gain the most understanding of the valuation process, use more than one method and compare the results. It's likely that you will get different results using the various methods—that's expected. Each method sheds some light on how investors view early stage startup valuations, better preparing you for valuation discussions and due diligence.

Experienced entrepreneurs use structured methods to come up with valuations because the structure provides a basis to share and sell the value of the startup's accomplishments and capabilities. In contrast, simply pulling a valuation number out of the air leaves you speechless when confronted with the question "How did you arrive at this valuation?"

Share Price Comes Later

When working through valuation calculations and discussions with your cofounders, advisors, and investors, think and discuss in the total dollar value of valuation, not in the price per share. The price per share is determined AFTER the valuation is established, not before.

The Market Comp Valuation Method

One of the quickest ways to establish a valuation for your startup is to compare it to another startup that has already closed a funding deal, and therefore negotiated its valuation with the equity investors.

Valuation comps, short for comparison, are often used by investors to get a quick estimate valuation for your startup. The thinking goes something like this:

> "You are like startup X and it was just valued at $1.5 million pre-money, so your startup must also be in that same pre-money range."

Added Benefit of Valuation Comps. Comps also provide additional validation for an investor. If other investors put money in the startup being used as a comparison to your startup, then it means the investors believe several things must be true. For example, the startup is in an large and growing market, the founders have enough experience to push the startup to success, the innovation or technology is proven with customers that pay, and so on. In short, valuation comps can give the investor some confidence, along this line of thought: "There are other startups out there getting funded like the one I'm considering, so perhaps my investment will be safe or even profitable."

The Market Comp method can also be used as a sanity check for other valuation methods. For example, you might use the Risk Mitigation method (detailed later) to log dozens of accomplishments and arrive at a solid pre-money valuation, then use the Market Comp method to validate and adjust your conclusions.

Method Overview

The Market Comp method is the most straight forward valuation methods—find a startup with a publicized valuation that closely compares to your startup—same stage of development, similar team, similar market segment, and similar technology or unique offering. Simply use the valuation of the comp startup as a basis for your valuation.

Experienced investors operating in areas of the country with high startup activity, such as Silicon Valley, use market comps to establish initial valuation ranges for negotiations with startups.

Market Comp Method, Step by Step

1. ***Create a short profile of your startup.*** List the factors that describe your startup, including stage of development, target markets, technology approach, and customer traction. A profile might look like this:

Startup Attributes	**Your Startup**
Industry:	Mobile
Niche:	App discovery
Founder Experience:	First-time startup founders
Company Location:	Boston, MA
Customer Traction:	3 paying early adopters
B2B or B2C:	B2B
Stage of Development:	Early - MVP launched
Funding:	Personal & F&F: $100,000
Team:	Still recruiting
Valuation:	TBD

39

2. *Find similar startups with known valuations to use as comps.* Several websites and startup blogs offer detailed information about startups and their funding successes. Use these sites to find startups similar to yours:

- AngelList (www.angel.co)

- CrunchBase (www.crunchbase.com)

- Hacker News (www.news.ycombinator.com/news)

- Gust (www.gust.com)

  Once you've located a startup to use as a comp, create a quick list of the startup's attributes similar to the list you created in step 1, and note the valuation established for the comp.

Don't Bring Me Down

Don't be discouraged by the impressively high valuations you see on sites like AngelList. A large percentage of the startups sharing their funding details on these sites are located in startup heavy areas of the country such as Silicon Valley and are well beyond the early stages of startup development. Even startups in less investor-rich areas of the country have been successful in raising capital from investors. Be sure to search or sort the startups you find on AngelList for the Seed stage to find startups that are truly considered early stage.

3. **Compare your startup profile to the comp's profile.** Once you've found one or two startups that are similar to yours, make notes to compare them in detail to the profile you created in Step 1. Here's what a comp comparison might look like:

Your Startup	Startup Attributes	Comp Startup
Mobile	Industry	Mobile
App discovery	Niche	Search
First-time startup founders	Founder Experience	1 experienced, 2 new co-founders
Boston, MA	Company Location	New York, NY
3 paying early adopters	Customer Traction	2 Ad network mid-sized
B2B	B2B or B2C	B2B
Early - MVP launched	Stage of Development	Early - Version 1.2 released
Personal & F&F: $100,000	Funding	Seed: $250,000
Still recruiting	Team	Core team onboard
TBD	Valuation	$2,200,000

4. **Adjust the comp valuation for large and obvious differences.** It can be difficult to find comp startups that align perfectly with your startup. Some comparison factors have a minor impact on the validity of the comp. Other factors, such as stage of development have a major impact on the alignment of the comp. If you find a good comp where most of the comp factors match except for one for one or two, adjust the valuation up or down to compensate for the difference. Remember, it's not an exact science, so use your best judgment and make a note why you made the adjustment—you are likely to need to defend the valuation with potential investors.

Short Discussions

For experienced investors and founders, reaching an agreeable pre-money valuation can be quick work. Contrary to some perceptions, most startup valuations are not hotly negotiated over months of back and forth point counter-point volleys. Investors know their limits and founders know they need to focus on the bigger end game beyond the perfect valuation and minimal dilution.

Market Comp Considerations

While the market comp valuation method is a fast path to setting a valuation, be sure to keep these considerations in mind as you experiment with the method:

Use More Than One. Don't rely on a Market Comp as the only basis for your valuation. While a close match to your startup is a good validation for investor discussions, using additional valuation methods (such as the Step Up, Risk Mitigation, and VC methods described later) will give you more ammunition to use in justifying your valuation with investors.

Heavy Startup Activity. Establishing a valuation based on comps is most practical in geographical areas where lots of angel and VC investing is taking place, like Silicon Valley, Boston, or New York. These startup-rich areas give rise to enough deals to provide a wide variety of deals, providing a larger pool of potential comps for various types of startups. In other areas of the country, less active deal flow may make it tougher for founders and investors to find enough similar startups to reference for valuations.

Head to Head Comps. If you find a head to head competitor (competing for the same customers as you), you can still use its valuation as a basis for your valuation, but you'd better spend some time determining how you will differentiate your startup in the market and in the eyes of investors. Be ready to explain how you are going to compete with the comp startup, considering factors such as:

- Your team

- Your ability to execute

- Technology and IP

- Market timing

- Funding plan

The Step Up Valuation Method

Startup founders often take inventory of their accomplishments to measure their progress and plan their next goals and milestones. The Step Up valuation method offers a structured way to use these accomplishments and external validations (such as customer traction) to develop a pre-money valuation.

Method Overview

The experts at 1x1 Media created the Step Up valuation method specifically for this guide. Fast and easy to follow, this method uses yes or no questions to arrive at a pre-money valuation, and is granular enough to be defensible when negotiating with investors. The key aspects of the method include:

- **Inspired by the Berkus Method.** The Step Up valuation method presented here is inspired by the Dave Berkus approach (Tech Coast Angels – Southern California). The original model created by Berkus avoids the need to rely on, or debate, a founder's financial forecasts, but instead, it loosely quantifies other major factors that strongly influence a startup's valuation and chance of success. Berkus's method considers the following factors and valuation amounts:

Characteristic	Add to Pre-Money Valuation
1. Quality of Management Team	$0 to $500,000
2. Sound Idea	$0 to $500,000
3. Working Prototype	$0 to $500,000
4. Quality Board of Directors	$0 to $500,000
5. Product Rollout or Sales	$0 to $500,000
Total Pre-Money Valuation	$0 to $2,500,000

- **Step-Up Model - 10 Valuation Factors.** The Step Up method detailed here includes 10 valuation factors and builds on the Berkus model by adding factors related to the startup founders' progress toward validating the startup's product or service with customers, as well as two founder-related factors: previous exit experience and more than one founder working in the startup full time. These additional factors are at the center of any discussion with experienced investors, so we feel they should be considered in any valuation estimation.

- **$250,000 for Each Yes.** Using the Step-Up model is simple: each Yes checked off in the factors list earns you another $250,000 in pre-money valuation, with a maximum of $2.5 million (a common limit for most investors considering early-stage startups.)

Step Up Method, Step by Step

The following steps illustrate how to use the Step Up

valuation model to calculate a pre-money valuation for your startup:

1. **Rate your startup on the 10 Step Up valuation factors.** Each factor that you can confidently say yes to gets a checkmark.

Step Up Factor	Yes
1. Total market size over $500,000,000	✔
2. Business model scales well	✔
3. Founders have previous exits or significant experience	
4. More than one founder comitted full time	✔
5. MVP developed, customer development underway	✔
6. Business model validated by paying customers	
7. Significant industry partnerships signed	
8. Execution roadmap developed and being achieved	✔
9. IP issued or technology protected	✔
10. Competitive environment favorable	
Total	6

2. **Calculate your total pre-money valuation.** Add $250,000 for each Yes you scored on the 10 Step Up factors. This chart illustrates the process.

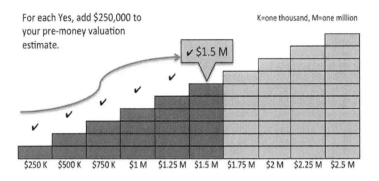

For each Yes, add $250,000 to your pre-money valuation estimate.

K=one thousand, M=one million

✔ $1.5 M

$250 K $500 K $750 K $1 M $1.25 M $1.5 M $1.75 M $2 M $2.25 M $2.5 M

Step Up Considerations

As with all early-stage valuation methods there is a good deal of subjectivity to each of the step up factors. Take into account the following considerations when working with the Step Up method:

Substitute Factors in the List. Feel free to substitute or add a factor to the list if you think it has significant impact on your valuation, and is defensible in the eyes of investors. For example, many investors favor startups that have attracted a notable board of directors (BOD), so this might be a factor to substitute in the list.

All-or-None Factors. Some investors may consider some factors an all-or-none deal point. For example, some angel groups heavily favor technology protected by issued patents and opt not to invest at all if there is no intellectual property (IP). Or equally common, many investors place having paying customers that validate your product's value and business model in the must-have category. The good news is that if you are negotiating (not merely discussing) your valuation with an investor, then that person has already crossed the "should I invest?" hurdle and you can focus on reaching a fair deal and putting some money in the bank.

Partial Credit. If you choose, you can issue yourself partial credit for each factor in the list, assigning a dollar value in the range from $0 to $250,000 (the Berkus method also allows for relative credits in the various categories).

There are No Rules

As you might conclude, there are not exact formulas or even universally accepted methods for establishing early-stage startup valuations. No matter which method you use, or if you derive your own model, be sure that the resulting valuation can be easily explained, and is in alignment with the facts of your startup.

Risk Mitigation Valuation Method

As your startup accomplishes tasks, such as launching an early version of your product, signing up paying customers, attracting experienced team members, or filing for a patent, the risk in the startup is being reduced. Consequently, the valuation of the startup grows. The Risk Mitigation method uses this idea to develop a robust basis for your pre-money valuation estimate.

Method Overview

The Risk Mitigation method assigns dollar values to the accomplishments and validations of the startup in four categories of risk mitigation: Technology, Market, Execution, and Capital.

The values assigned to the accomplishments represent either actual dollars spent to achieve the task or estimations of the "worth or value" of the item/outcome. For example, you might spend $25,000 to build a working prototype of your product (logged as actual dollars spent in the Technology category), or assign a value of $100,000 to your successful early adopter customers (logged as the perceived value of the accomplishment in the Market category.)

From an investor's point of view, the four risk mitigation categories can be summarized by asking the following questions:

> **Technology.** Does your product work as planned? Can it be manufactured or deployed to the market at a cost that supports your business model? Have you started building layers of protection around the technology with patents or trade secrets?

> **Market.** Do customers care about your product or

service? Are they willing to pay for it? Is the size of the market large enough to support your projections as well as fend off inevitable competitors?

Execution. Is your team experienced in the segment you are targeting? Do founders have previous startup experience? Do you have a track record of clear ability to execute the plans you set forth? Are you able to attract key employees needed to fill gaps and grow the startup?

Capital. Have the founders invested personal funds to move the startup from idea to reality? Have you raised Friends and Family funding, showing others are willing to place a bet on your venture? Do you have a funding plan that outlines key milestones, funds needed, and contingency plans? How many funding rounds are likely to be needed to reach breakeven?

This example shows of what a risk mitigation valuation build up might look like.

Technology Risk Mitigation

- Prototype developed: $75,000

- 3rd party testing completed: $25,000

- IP underway: $25,000

Market Risk Mitigation

- Market research: $20,000

- Early adopter program in place: $100,000

- Channel partners established: $40,000

Execution Risk Mitigation

- Experienced founders, previous startups: $200,000

- Prior exit: $250,000

- Detailed execution roadmap in place: $50,000

Capital Risk Mitigation

- Early funding (friends and family): $50,000

- Only two angel rounds needed: $100,000

Add up all the values to get a pre-money valuation, $935,000 in this example.

A Risk Mitigation valuation offers the advantage of summing many smaller elements or small victories. An investor can argue that one number in the valuation list is too high, but since that number might be a small piece of the total valuation, the impact of lowering the line item value impacts the total valuation less.

Risk Mitigation Valuation, Step by Step

1. ***Create a list of all the accomplishments of your startup.*** Create an exhaustive list of all the tasks you have achieved to date. Use the following categories to help stimulate your memory.

   Money. Things you've spent money on or other financial equivalents such as founder salaries foregone at day jobs.

   Travel. Places you've traveled to meet with customers, suppliers, partners, or industry events.

   People. Relationships developed with employees, advisors, experts, investors, and customers.

51

Exposure. Keynote speeches, press coverage, blog write-ups, social and web rankings.

Events. Tradeshows, industry conferences, customer forums, in-store demos, and sponsorships.

Design. Product design, branding, web and mobile design, software algorithms, user interfaces, and packaging.

Process. Sales process, business models, market approach, order flow, and customer acquisition.

Metrics. Customer lifetime value, conversion rates, cost to acquire, cost per employee, burn rate, churn.

2. *Place each accomplishment in one of the four risk mitigation categories: Technology, Market, Execution, and Capital.* If you are not sure where an item falls, drop it in somewhere and make a note. This is not an exact science, but rather a thoughtful structure to derive an approximate pre-money valuation.

3. *Assign a value to each task/accomplishment in the list.* Big achievements get big values. For example, paying customers that keep coming back is perhaps one of the biggest achievements and should contribute a large dollar value to your valuation.

4. *Apply value multipliers where needed.* Some accomplishments are worth more (in valuation terms) than the actual dollars received or spent on them. For example, let's say an early customer has been using your service for six months and paying $99 per month. Such a huge validation is worth more than a mere $600 in valuation. A more meaningful measure of the paying customer is the Lifetime Value of the

monthly payments; say 10 years x $99 per month or $12,000. Start with a factual dollar value and apply defendable multipliers to increase the value of the accomplishment.

5. **Add it up.** Add up all of the values in your list to result in a total pre-money valuation.

Risk Mitigation Considerations

Because it's based on the numerous accomplishments and validations checked off your company building list, the Risk Mitigation Valuation method is one of the more easily defended valuation techniques when negotiating with investors. That said; keep the following additional factors in mind as you work toward establishing a valuation using the method.

> **Sanity Check.** Take a second look at the elements in your risk mitigation valuation list. If needed, make adjustments to bring the valuation into a range that fits with the overall stage of your startup. If the total valuation adds up to be quite low and yet you have a long list of real accomplishments, perhaps you are under valuing the key items on your list. Conversely, if you are at the early idea stage of your startup and arrive at a valuation of more than $1,000,000, you might be over optimistic about the value of the items on your list. Remember, experienced investors have seen many deals and have a general expectation of how similar companies are valued.

> **Technology Development Dollars.** One tricky question facing founders is deciding how much value to place on Research and Development (R&D) dollars invested by the startup.

For example, consider a startup that develops new medical device hardware. They have spent millions of dollars developing a working prototype. The startup received large government grants to help fund the R&D effort. Shouldn't all this investment be accounted for in our valuation? Maybe Yes, Maybe no.

From the investor's point of view, money invested in your startup for technology development does not necessarily mean you warrant a valuation that accounts for all of that investment.

The following examples show factors supporting R&D dollars in a valuation build up:

New Innovations with Big Markets. The value of any new innovation hinges on the market acceptance of the product, how big that market is, how that market is growing and the ease of reaching the customers in that market.

Revolutionary Products. One way to think about large R&D investments is to ask this question: "Does the heavy R&D investment result in a innovation that is revolutionary or merely evolutionary?" If the result is only a slightly better product (evolutionary), then investors don't give much weight to the R&D invested dollars.

Significant Barrier to Entry. Does the R&D investment result in a significant barrier to entry, making it much more difficult for other competitors to duplicate your product. Investors place a high value on new technology that is hard for competitors to copy.

These factors provide example that make it difficult to justify large R&D investments in valuation build up:

Our Version of the Same Thing. The R&D effort results in your version of something that already exists.

Innovation without a Market. The R&D funding was unfocused on solving a particular market need. Innovation driven by the desire to explore a field with little or no regard to how the technology might be commercialized is not highly valued by most investors. While this kind of research helps move the "how the world works" ball forward, investors tend to heavily discount any investments made in relationship to a pre-money valuation.

The VC Quick Valuation Method

The VC Quick valuation method illustrates how quickly an investor can size up your startup and consequently, their estimation of what your valuation "should" be. Unlike more detailed build up methods like the Risk Mitigation method, this method jumps to the answer with only a few inputs.

Here's how it works.

Method Overview

The method starts with the startup articulating their funding needs for the next 18 months.

"At our current burn rate, we need $3 million for the next 18 months. This level of funding gets us to significant milestones, creating the validations we need to raise the next round of funding."

The VC knows that to get involved, they want to own at least 20% of the company. Anything significantly less will not be worth their time. With the raise amount and VC ownership percentages known, the valuation is settled.

VC Quick Valuation, Step by Step

The following example demonstrates how the VCs will answer the valuation question for themselves.

1. *How much money do you need for the next 18 months?* Let's say you respond that $3 million dollars are needed to fund your operations for the next 18 months.

Raise Amount

$3 Million

Covers the Next

18 Months

2. ***Understand how much equity the VCs want.*** The VCs know they want to own at least 20% equity in your venture. Anything less isn't worthwhile for that level of investment. Anything significantly more would likely be too dilutive for founders and existing shareholders.

Desired Equity

20%

Ownership

3. ***Calculate the post-money valuation.*** The $3 million raise amount divided by the desired equity ownership of 20% (expressed as a decimal) results in the company's post-money valuation of $15 million.

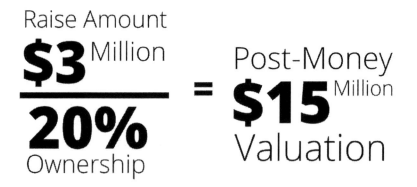

Raise Amount $3 Million / 20% Ownership = Post-Money $15 Million Valuation

4. **Calculate the resulting pre-money valuation.** With the post-money valuation known, calculate the pre-money valuation as follows:

Post-Money $15 Million Valuation - Raise Amount $3 Million = Pre-Money $12 Million Valuation

That's it. Of course, there are many other fundraising deal factors that are important to both founders and VC investors—liquidation preferences, anti-dilution provisions, and board seats. All of these factors have a big impact on how founders are affected by the investment deal—the valuation question is only one factor.

VC Quick Considerations

The method is best suited for startups that have the following attributes:

Developed Product/Service and Paying Customers. The startup had moved past the early stages of product development and customer discovery.

Quality Metrics. You and your startup team have a good understanding of the key metrics that drive your business. For example, you know the cost to acquire each customer, what your customer churn rate is, what the lifetime value of a typical customer is.

Stable Operation and Complete Team. There are no major gaps in your startup leadership team. Other team roles are filled with great people and your day-to-day operation is well defined.

Funding Needs Are Well Understood. You know how much money you need to raise in your current round, and the uses of funds need to be clear and predicable.

As you can see, the VC Quick Method is not well suited for very early-stage startups. There are still too many guesses. You cannot estimate your burn rate per month. Your team is not filled out or stable. The cost to acquire customers is still being tested and so on. That said, as a well-rounded founder, keep the VC Quick method in mind as you work to raise the funding you need.

The VC Valuation Method

Unlike the VC "Quick" method and other valuation methods outlined here, this VC Valuation method relies on a few financial assumptions and totally ignores factors such as founder experience, customer traction, and milestone achievement. (These factors do come into play when the VC is deciding whether to invest or not, however.)

Venture capitalists invest in new ventures as a profession, investing large amounts of other institution's money (university foundations, private equity holdings, etc.) To this professional investment goal, VCs are expected to show large returns on the cash invested in the startups in their portfolio. The VC valuation method uses this ROI expectation to derive a pre-money valuation for the startup.

Method Overview

The VC valuation method was originally described in a case study by Harvard Business School Professor William A. Sahlman. The method centers on the idea of deriving what your pre-money valuation needs to be to satisfy the expected return on investment required by the angels or VCs you are negotiating with. The following points outline the method:

- **Starts at the End and Work Backwards.** The VC method starts with the end game in mind—the acquisition (or exit) of the startup. An exit value (the amount your startup is being acquired for) is assumed, and then worked backward to calculate what your startup must be worth now based on that exit value and expected ROI.

- **Puts Financial Projections in Play.** This method uses financial projections of the startup, specifically annual revenues in the year of the startup's exit, and can also include use of public company data for P/E (Price/Earnings) multiples. This approach is not used for early-stage startups, but rather ones with at least a couple of years of full operation, and is making predictable earning/profits.

- **Incorporates Return on Investment (ROI) Expectations.** Professional investors like VCs establish return on investment hurdles for the startups being evaluated. If the VCs don't think the startup can achieve the hurdle ROI (20 times the investment amount for example), then they don't invest. The VC valuation method uses an ROI expectation to work backward from the future exit of the startup, deriving a current pre-money valuation.

VC Method, Step by Step

1. *Understand the equation.* Your goal in this method is to work backward from the exit event of the startup, first determining what your current post-money valuation would have to be in order to satisfy the investor's desired return on investment (ROI) multiple. This equation below shows how these parameters are connected. The amount your startup gets acquired for in say five to seven years, divided by your current post-money valuation, gives the ROI multiple—hopefully in the 10X to 20X range to satisfy the large returns targeted by experienced investors.

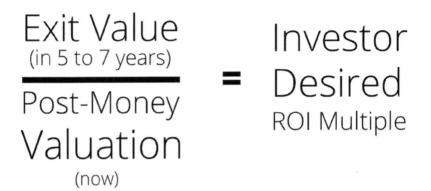

$$\frac{\text{Exit Value (in 5 to 7 years)}}{\text{Post-Money Valuation (now)}} = \text{Investor Desired ROI Multiple}$$

Next, flip the equation around to focus on the post-money target:

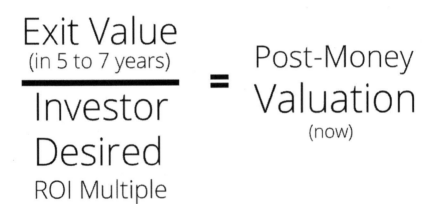

$$\frac{\text{Exit Value (in 5 to 7 years)}}{\text{Investor Desired ROI Multiple}} = \text{Post-Money Valuation (now)}$$

2. **Estimate your exit value.** To solve the equation outlined in Step 1 above, we need to estimate how much the startup can be sold for in its exit year. There are two common ways to make a guess about your exit value.

Simple exit value estimation using industry trends.
Say you know startups in your space typically get
acquired for two times (2X) their annual revenues. For
example, if you expect your exit year annual revenues
will be $20 million, then your startup's exit value
would be $40 million.

$$\underset{\text{2X}}{\underset{\text{Multiple}}{\text{Exit}}} \times \underset{\text{\$20 Million}}{\underset{\text{Revenue}}{\text{Exit Year}}} = \underset{\text{\$40 Million}}{\text{Exit Value}}$$

**More complex exit value estimation using Price/
Earnings multiples.** Using Price/Earnings multiples
for your industry/space, you calculate your exit
value.

For example, you:

- Know companies in your space have P/E ratios of
  10.

- Estimate your before tax earnings to be 16% of
  your revenues (also referred to as Return on Sales,
  or ROS).

- Estimate your Year five annual revenues will be
  $25 million.

Using these parameters, calculate your earnings in
your exit year (year five in this example), and then
multiply by the P/E multiplier to get an exit value, as
follows. In our example, a P/E of 10 multiplied by our
$4 million earnings estimate, gives a final exit value of
$40 millions dollars.

$$\underset{\text{16\%}}{\text{ROS \%}} \quad \times \quad \underset{\substack{\text{Revenue}\\\text{\$25 Million}}}{\text{Exit Year}} \quad = \quad \underset{\text{\$4 Million}}{\text{Earnings}}$$

$$\underset{\text{10}}{\text{P/E Multiplier}} \quad \times \quad \underset{\text{\$4 Million}}{\text{Earnings}} \quad = \quad \underset{\text{\$40 Million}}{\text{Exit Value}}$$

3. **Calculate the post-money valuation.** Now with your startup's exit value estimated, you can calculate what your post-money valuation would have to be (now) to meet the investors' desired return on investment.

You know:

- Your estimated exit value is $40 million (from Step 2)

- You know that investors are hoping for a 20 times (20X) return on their investment

Therefore your current post-money valuation needs to be $2 million.

$$\frac{\underset{\text{ROI Multiple}}{\underset{\text{20}}{\underline{\text{Exit Value}\ \text{\$40 Million}}}}}{} \quad = \quad \underset{\text{\$2 Million}}{\text{Post-Money Valuation}}$$

4. ***Calculate your pre-money valuation.*** Using the amount of the current investment round you can easily calculate what your current pre-money valuation is:

You know:

- You are trying to raise $500,000 from the investors

- Your target post-money valuation needs to be $2 million from Step 3

- Therefore, your pre-money valuation is $1.5 million

Post-Money Valuation **$2 Million** – Investment Amount **$500,000** = Post-Money Valuation **$1.5 Million**

5. ***Calculate the equity percentage owned by the investors.*** Finally, divide the $500,000 investment amount by the post-money valuation to get the amount of equity that would be owned by the investor.

Investment Amount **$500,000** / $2 Million Post-Money Valuation = Investor Ownership **25%**

In summary, if you are raising $500,000 now, your pre-money valuation needs to be $1.5 million, and your startup needs to get acquired for $40 million (or more) in order for investors to get their desired 20X multiple on their money. (Note that this is a simplified example. Many other Term Sheet deal factors influence how much an investor gets from the sale proceeds of an exit event.)

VC Method Considerations

Slogging though the math of the VC valuation method should be concluded with the following two considerations.

One Big Assumption. The VC method relies on the idea that you can estimate the exit value of your startup several years into the future. If your pre-money valuation is based on the idea that you could get acquired for $40 million in the future, and investors have trouble believing this exit value is possible, you are left with little room to negotiate. You can argue points that support the exit value, but little else. As mentioned before, don't rely on just one valuation method, but rather experiment with several to discover better and more detailed justifications for you starting number.

Understanding the VC Mindset. One of the side benefits of experimenting with the VC method for early-stage founders is that it sheds light on how VCs think about investments. In short, the startup must be able to exit for X dollars within Y years, and the VCs require a 20X return on investment. If any part of the this high hurdle equation breaks down, then the VCs will not invest.

3

Option Pool Impact on Valuation

It is common for institutional investors such as VCs to require the startup to establish a stock incentive plan in the form of stock options. (Earlier stage investors such as Angel groups are less concerned with the stock option pool topic.)

This section details the potential impact of option pool creation on your valuation negotiations with investors.

True Pre-Money Valuation

Also referred to as *effective valuation* or the *option pool shuffle*. True pre-money valuation is a term that refers to the effect on your pre-money valuation when you create a stock option pool out of the founder's equity, prior to any funding being injected by new investors.

The option pool can be created either pre-money, or post-money. Pre-money pool creation carves out the option pool from the founder's equity, before the investment round. Post-money creation carves out the option pool from the combined equity of the founders and investors, after the investment round has been completed.

If the option pool is designated to be created "pre-money", then the founders pay for the entire option pool out of their own pocket (of equity).

Consider this scenario that shows the basis for the *true pre-money* term:

You negotiate your pre-money valuation with investors, say $2,000,000. Term sheet negotiations go well, but the term sheet drafted by the investors includes the clause:

> "the Company's pre-money valuation includes a reserve 20% of its Common Stock shares, on a fully diluted basis, to be available for future issuances to directors, officers, employees, and consultants."

The effect of this term sheet clause effectively lowers your pre-money valuation by $400,000, 20% of the negotiated pre-money valuation (.20 x $2,000,000), resulting in a true pre-money valuation of $1,600,00, rather than your expected $2,000,000

True Pre-Money Valuation Math

These steps show the true pre-money valuation calculations.

1. ***Review the current parameters of your fundraising discussions with investors.*** In this case, say the founders have agreed on a pre-money valuation of $2 million, a raise amount of $500,000, and investors are asking for a 20% option pool to be created pre-money.

Negotiated Pre-Money	**$2,000,000**
+ Raise Amount	**$500,000**
Post-Money Valuation	**$2,500,000**

Investor Ownership %	**20%**

(Raise Amount / Post-Money Valuation)

2. Calculate the dollar value of the option pool.

With the investment deal points understood, first calculate the dollar value of the proposed 20% pre-money option pool. Simply multiply the option pool percentage (expressed as a decimal) by the agreed on pre-money valuation.

Required Option Pool %	**20%**
× Negotiated Pre-Money	**$2,000,000**
Option Pool Dollar Value	**$400,000**

3. Calculate the true pre-money valuation.

Subtracting the option pool dollar value from the negotiated pre-money valuation results in the true pre-money valuation.

Negotiated Pre-Money	**$2,000,000**
− Option Pool Value	**$400,000**
True Pre-Money	**$1,600,000**

4. Recalculate the equity ownership percentage that will be owned by the investors. Add the raise amount to the true pre-money valuation, resulting in the true post-money valuation. Divide the raise amount by the true post-money valuation to give the true investor ownership percentage.

True Pre-Money	**$1,600,000**
+ Raise Amount	**$500,000**
True Post- Money	**$2,100,000**

Investor Ownership %	**24%**
(Raise Amount / True Post-Money)	

With a clear picture of the valuation and equity ownership numbers, founders can work with the investors to resolve any differences. Options for tweaking the terms of an investment deal include **agreeing on a higher pre-money valuation** that offsets the impact of the pre-money option pool or asking the investors to share in the impact of the option pool by **creating the option pool based on the post-money valuation** and ownership picture.

4

How to Respond to Investor Questions About Your Valuation

Your Valuation Is Too High

Investors that tell you that your valuation is "too high" typically have more detailed reasons for their statement. Here are several examples that reveal what investor might be really saying.

> **Investment Fund Criteria.** Too high, meaning "your valuation is above the limit of our fund criteria. We only invest in startups with a valuation of 2 million or less." Many angel investment funds and networks only entertain pitches from startups that are early-stage with valuations below certain limits. A high valuation is usually almost always linked to a high raise amount. Be sure to ask the angels if they have such criteria.

> **More Equity.** Too high, meaning, "we like your startup and team and we'd like to talk about an investment, but we'd like to get a bit more equity to offset the risk of the investment." This is the conversation you want to have. Too high often means "let's talk more."

More Control. Too high, meaning, "this is a negotiation and you need to give on some elements of the deal." If founders are flexible on other deal terms such as preferred share rights like voting and board seats, investors might be willing to accept a higher valuation.

Your Revenues Don't Support Your Valuation

It's not uncommon for startup founders to hear this feedback from some angel investors. To understand their perspective, let's take a look at a more detailed example of this challenge.

Early-stage, Low Revenues Scenario. You use the risk mitigation valuation method to arrive at a valuation of $1.5 million dollars based on all of the accomplishments you've achieved so far. You pitch a local angel investment group and in the final slide of your pitch, you review your next steps and relate that are working on raising a total of $250,000 to support your next stage of growth.

After your pitch, one of the investors asks what your monthly revenues have been for the last 3 months. You respond between $8000 and $12,000. If you multiply these revenue averages by 12, your current annual revenues would be around $120,000.

The angel investors says, "well, how can you place a value of $1.5 million when you are only making $10 grand a month? At best, you are only worth $250,000!"

Here's how to respond:

1. "Our valuation estimate is based on many factors, with current revenue run rates being only one of them."

2. "While our current revenues are relatively low, they are a clear validation of the market opportunity for our company."

3. "We believe our ability to execute, our large target market size, and our proven and passionate customer base all support our valuation target."

4. "We value your input and would love to review our valuation assumptions in more detail with you."

So how is this investor arriving at such a low valuation?

An investor focused on revenue or profit projections as the primary basis for valuation is likely experienced with the Discounted Cash Flow (DCF) idea of valuing an investment. While DCF is an accepted method for later stage, more mature companies, it is not well suited for early stage startups. See the section "Understanding Accounting Valuation Methods" for more details.

Investors that require that your current and recent past revenues to completely support the valuation you propose are not willing to take as much risk as other early stage investors.

So, no, your actual revenues do not need to tie directly to your valuation estimate. Of course you can build a set of financial projections that show how you'll grow your revenues rapidly, and therefore support a Discounted Cash Flow valuation model. But as many investors say, "Anybody can make money in Excel". If you encounter such investors, keep pitching to other investors until you find someone who values other intangible valuation factors, such as customer or user acceptance of your product/service.

You're Too Early

Angels do a good job vetting the startups that request to pitch to the investor group, but sometimes founders get the feedback from the investors that the startup is "too early". "You don't need angel investors yet. We think you are over valuing your startup for the stage and validations you have. We think there are too many unknowns right now. Come back to pitch us again when you have more users, paying customers, IP locked down, etc."

Savvy founders faced with "too early" feedback from angel investors take the feedback with grace and shift gears and use other sources of funding to grow their ventures. Friends and family loans, small business loans from Community Development

Financial Institutions (CDFI's), and cash flow from the business itself are common sources.

If you are confronted with the "Too Early" comment, take the feedback constructively and be sure to ask the investors for their ideas and counsel, and then request to pitch them again when you have removed more risk from your startup venture.

5

Understanding Accounting Valuation Methods

Talk with a CPA or company accountant about business valuation and you'll hear terms such as *discounted cash flow, earnings multiples*, and *discretionary cash flow*. Accountants use these and other procedures to evaluate the financial condition, performance, and ultimately place a valuation on a business—key point, well established businesses.

Quantitative Valuation Models

Accounting-based methods are called quantitative because they depend on evaluating the financial reports of the business over a multi-year timeframe.

Startups Need Not Apply. As you might be guessing, quantitative valuation methods are not useful for early-stage startups. Why? Quantitative valuation models depend on several years of financial reports as well as forward-looking forecasts. It is not uncommon for a valuation specialist to review three to five years of historical financial reports using the past financial performance to derive revenue and cash flow projections to arrive at a business valuation. Clearly, early-stage startups do not have such financial history to support an accounting based valuation.

Accounting Valuations Distilled

The following summaries provide an overview of quantitative methods. A quick review shows why these methods do not work for early-stage startups.

> **Discounted Cash Flow (DCF).** Using this method, the current value of the company is estimated using future cash flow projections and discounting (adjusting down) the value of those cash flows. As you may recall, having money now is worth more than money in the future. For the accountant or valuation professional to build accurate future cash flows guesses, they look to the past cash flow performance of the company—the more years available, the better. The DCF method also depends on accurate cash flow projections—something difficult for early stage startups to predict.

> **Earnings Multiplier Models.** Earnings multiple valuation methods compare well established earnings metrics of similar companies in a particular industry and assume similar multipliers apply to your company. This method depends on historical stock prices and earnings data from a relatively large number of peer companies, typically publicly traded companies operating in very similar business segments. These methods can reveal connections such as, "Companies like yours are valued at 12 times your earnings per share." Early-stage startups rarely have revenue and associated earnings needed to for this quantitative method to be a valid measure of the valuation goal.

> **Asset-Based Valuations.** This valuation method derives a valuation by adding the total asset value of items including land, property, and equipment, and then subtracting the liabilities of the company. Clearly, this is not a good model for new or growing businesses with very few if any hard assets. It does not take into account the future earnings potential of the business, or other difficult to value items such as patents, code, or brand or market recognition.

6

Understanding 409A Valuations

Read enough startup blogs or hang out at entrepreneurial gatherings long enough and you will likely encounter the phrase *"409A valuation."* Luckily, this jargon is not something early-stage founders need to worry about, at least not at the formation stage of their ventures. But as soon as your startup establishes a stock incentive plan and issues stock options to employees or other stakeholders, it's time to dig in and address the 409A valuation topic.

The Stock Option Valuation. A 409A valuation is not a true valuation method in itself, but rather the reason you get a valuation performed for your startup. If your startup has established a stock option plan to reward employees with a portion of equity ownership in the company, a 409A valuation is somewhere in you future.

The U.S. tax code (section 409A) requires private companies show that their common stock options are issued at fair market value. Employees, founders, and other stakeholders are taxed on the value of the stock options they own and to avoid potential tax penalties, the startup must get a formal valuation opinion at least once every 12 months.

To calculate the value of the stock options, a value (called fair market value) must be established for the company stock each year. As the company grows, the stock hopefully becomes more valuable, and so do the stock options.

CPAs and other experienced valuation experts use accounting or quantitative methods to establish a 409A triggered valuation—earning multiples, discounted cash flow, and comps with other startups to name a few. As described earlier, these methods involve the detailed review of past financials, assessment and comparison to similar startups (comps), and review of the assets of the business including physical assets like equipment and buildings and intangible assets like patents and other IP.

Thank You

This concludes the *Founder's Pocket Guide: Startup Valuation 2nd Edition*. We hope you find our content and supporting tools useful for your startup journey.

We are always looking for feedback on our startup tools. If you have comments, feedback, or corrections, please send us a note.

info@1x1media.com

http://www.1x1media.com

End Notes:

AngelList (www.angel.co)

CrunchBase (www.crunchbase.com)

Hacker News (www.news.ycombinator.com/news)

Gust (www.gust.com)

Dave Berkus approach (Tech Coast Angels – Southern California, www.berkus.com)

The VC valuation method, William A. Sahlman. (http://hbr.org/product/A-Method-For-Valuing-High/an/288006-PDF-ENG)

#

"Money is like gasoline during a road trip. You don't want to run out of gas on your trip, but you're not doing a tour of gas stations."

- Tim O'Reilly, O'Reilly Media founder and CEO

93850873R00046